SPANISH
LIFEPAC SEV

CONTENTS

Authors: **Katherine Engle, B.A., M.A.**
                    Vicki Seeley Milunich, B.A., M.S. Ed.
Editor: Alan Christopherson, M.S.
Graphic Design: Kyle Bennett, Jennifer Davis,
                    Alpha Omega Staff

Alpha Omega Publications

Published by Alpha Omega Publications, Inc.
300 North McKemy Avenue, Chandler, Arizona 85226-2618

SPANISH 1: LIFEPAC 7

OBJECTIVES

When you have completed this LIFEPAC, you should be able to:

1. Recognize and apply the reflexive pronoun for a variety of situations, particularly to express personal care needs.

2. Use those weather expressions for spoken and written experiences in the language.

3. Expand your expression by learning how to form Spanish adverbs.

4. Identify things out by learning the demonstrative adjective.

5. Reinforce your knowledge of expressions of **tener** and **ir** by reviewing LIFEPAC 6.

I. PERSONAL CARE

Conversation

Maria:	Hoy estoy muy cansada.
Pablo:	¿Qué pasó?
Maria:	Anoche no me dormí hasta muy tarde. Vi una película fantástica en la televisión.
Pablo :	¿A qué hora te acuestas normalmente?
Maria:	Me acuesto a las nueve. Pero no me acosté hasta las once anoche.
Pablo :	¡Ay! ¿Y todavía te levantaste a las seis de la mañana?
Maria:	Hoy no. No me levanté hasta las siete y media. No tuve tiempo, y por eso no me duché, y no desayuné. ¡Solamente me peiné y me cepillé los dientes!
Pablo :	En vez de mirar la televisión debes hacer los ejercicios. Entonces te sientes mejor.
Maria:	Ya lo sé. ¿Puedes caminar conmigo después de la escuela?
Pablo :	Claro que sí. Por hacer los ejercicios, vas a sentirte mejor, dormir mejor y bajarte de peso. ¡Hasta las tres!
Maria:	¡Hasta luego!

Translation

Maria: Today I am very tired.

Pablo :   What happened?

Maria: Last night I didn't fall asleep until very late. I saw a great film on television.

Pablo :   What time do you normally go to bed?

Maria: I go to bed a 9:00. But I didn't go to bed last night until 11:00.

Pablo :   Wow! And you still got up a 6:00 this morning?

Maria;   Not today. I didn't get up until 7:30. I don't have time, and for that reason I didn't take a shower, I didn't eat breakfast. I only combed my hair and brushed my teeth!

Pablo :   Instead of watching television, you should do exercises. Then you will feel better.

Maria: I know that. Can you walk with me after school?

Pablo :   Of course. By doing exercises you're going to feel better, sleep better and lose weight. See you at 3:00!

Maria: See you later!

 Look through the conversation for forms of the following infinitives. List the forms under each.

1.1   dormirse   acostarse   levantarse   cepillarse

2

Using the translation as a guide, pick out the following Spanish words.

1.2   a. Teeth   _____

       b. I go to bed   _____

       c. You go to bed   _____

       d. I comb my hair   _____

       e. I take a shower   _____

       f. I feel   _____

       g. I do exercises   _____

       h. To lose weight   _____

       i. Of course   _____

       j. To walk   _____

 Conversation Practice

1.3   Practice the Spanish dialogue with a learning partner. Be ready to say it to the class or to an adult.

       ✔ Adult check _____
                                    Initial   Date

Here is a list of active vocabulary for personal care. Look over the list and practice it with a classmate.

1.4

el jabón – the soap
el champú – the shampoo
el cepillo – the brush
el cepillo de dientes – the toothbrush
el peine – the comb
la ducha – the shower
la bañera – the bathtub
la pasta dentífrica – the toothpaste
el espejo – the mirror
el maquillaje – the makeup
la secadora – the hair dryer
la ropa – the clothes
el zapato – the shoe
la toalla – the towel
el gimnasio – the gym
el desayuno – the breakfast
el almuerzo – the lunch
la cena – the supper
la cama – the bed
el dormitorio – the bedroom
el baño – the bathroom
el reloj – the clock
los dientes – the teeth
el pelo – the hair

✔ Adult check _____

Initial   Date

 Refer to the vocabulary list above and in the back of the LIFEPAC to complete this activity.

1.5   In the first blank, label the item in Spanish, being sure to include the articles (**el**, **la**, etc.). In the second blank, write a Spanish infinitive (action word) also chosen from the list.

a. _____   b. _____   c. _____   d. _____

_____   _____   _____   _____

4

e. _____   f. _____   g. _____   h. _____

_____   _____   _____   _____

i. _____   j. _____

_____   _____

Arrange the infinitives under the period of the day with which they are associated.

1.6   **LA MAÑANA**   **LA TARDE**   **LA NOCHE**

_____   _____   _____

_____   _____   _____

_____   _____   _____

Matching.

1.7   Complete as much of the matching as you can without looking at your vocabulary list. Use the list only to look up what you absolutely can't remember.

_____ 1. la bañera

_____ 2. el dormitorio

_____ 3. los zapatos

_____ 4. el peine

_____ 5. el espejo

_____ 6. el champú

_____ 7. la secadora

_____ 8. la ropa

_____ 9. el almuerzo

_____ 10. la ducha

SELF TEST 1

1.01   **Matching.** (3 pts. each)

_____ 1. to eat breakfast

_____ 2. to brush (one's hair/teeth)

_____ 3. to put on (oneself)

_____ 4. to get dressed (dress oneself)

_____ 5. to take off (oneself)

_____ 6. to leave, go out

_____ 7. to look at (oneself)

_____ 8. to go to bed

_____ 9. to comb (one's hair)

_____ 10. to wake (oneself) up

a. peinarse

b. irse

c. acostarse

d. desayunarse

e. cepillarse

f. vestirse

g. ponerse

h. despertarse

i. quitarse

j. mirarse

1.02   **Write the English:** (3 pts. each)

a. Bajarse del peso_____

b. Dormirse_____

c. Levantarse_____

d. Maquillarse_____

e. Ponerse a dieta _____

Write the Spanish: (3 pts. each)

f. to wash (oneself) _____

g. to gain weight _____

h. to shower (oneself) _____

i. to dry off _____

j. to sleep _____

1.03   **Yes or No – is this personal care item logically associated with the action given?** (3 pts. each)

a. _____ el maquillaje / maquillarse

b. _____ el jabón / dormirse

c. _____ la toalla / secarse

d. _____ el cereal / desayunarse

e. _____ los pesos / acostarse

f. _____ la alcoba / irse

g. _____ el espejo / mirarse

h. _____ los zapatos / quitarse

i. _____ la ropa / ponerse

j. _____ a hamburguesa / vestirse

72	
	90

Score   _____

Teacher check   _____
                 Initial   Date

7

II. GRAMMAR: REFLEXIVE VERBS

 Look at the following sentences and answer the questions below.

a. Yo baño al perro.

b. Yo me baño.

c. Yo cepillo al pelo
de mi hermanita.

d. Yo me cepillo el pelo.

2.1   To whom or for whom is the action being performed?

a. _____

b. _____

c. _____

d. _____

The activities pictured on the right (items b and d) are called a **reflexive action** because the subject (**yo**) is doing the bathing and combing to himself or herself. Think of a reflection in a mirror—an image of yourself is reflected or bounces right back to you. For example:

I see myself.   **He hurt himself.**   **We brush our teeth.**

2.2   Look at the Spanish sentences again, particularly the verbs. What is the difference between the
non-reflexive and the reflexive actions?

_____

Reflexive verbs are accompanied by special pronouns to tell the listener that the subject is performing the activity on himself or herself.

 Answer the following questions.

2.3   In the example **Yo me baño**, which word means "myself?" _____

2.4   Therefore, which word is the reflexive pronoun? _____

Now look at the forms of **bañarse** (to bathe yourself).

yo	me baño	nosostros	nos bañamos
tú	te bañas	vosotros	os bañáis
él	se baña	ellos	se bañan
ella	se baña	ellas	se bañan
Ud.	se baña	Uds.	se bañan

 Refer to the table above to answer these questions.

2.5   Which words are the reflexive pronouns?

    a. _____   d. _____

    b. _____   e. _____

    c. _____   f. _____

2.6   As we have established, **me** denotes "myself." What must the other pronouns denote?

    a. **me** _____   d. **nos** _____

    b. **te** _____   e. **se** _____

    c. **se** _____

2.7   Look at the verb **bañarse** again and write the forms that are left once the pronouns are removed (which you did above).

    a. _____   d. _____

    b. _____   e. _____

    c. _____   f. _____

By splitting the verb from the pronouns, we can see that a reflexive verb is a basic verb form with a pronoun added to it. For this reason, any Spanish infinitive can be made into a reflexive verb. For example, take the infinitive **mirarse** (to look at yourself). Draw a vertical line between **mirar** and **se**.

For each form, imagine physically moving that pronoun to the front (as you change it to agree with the new subjects). All that is left to do is conjugate the infinitive **mirar**, as shown below.

yo	me miro	nts	nos miramos
tú	te miras	vts	os miráis
él	se mira	ellos	se miran
ella	se mira	ellas	se miran
Ud.	se mira	Ustedes	se miran

If **miro** means "I look at" and **me** means "myself," then **me miro** must translate as "I look at myself."

 Complete the translations for the rest of the forms below.

2.8   a. yo me miro   _____

           b. tú te miras   _____

           c. él se mira   _____

           d. ella se mira   _____

           d. Usted se mira   _____

           f. Nosotros nos miramos   _____

           g. ellos se miran   _____

           h. ellas se miran   _____

           i. Ustedes se miran   _____

Furthermore, take note where the reflexive pronouns are placed. You see the **se** at the end of the infinitives (in the vocabulary list) but the **me**, **te**, etc. in front of the forms. There are two options for pronoun placement:

1. IN FRONT of a verb FORM

2. AFTER an infinitive

To understand more fully, look at the following pairs of sentences:

Nos vestimos por la mañana.   Me pongo a dieta.
Vamos a vestirnos por la mañana.   Voy a ponerme a dieta.

Te vas conmigo.   Se miran en el espejo.
Puedes irte conmigo?   A él le gusta mirarse en el espejo.

Ejercicio.

2.9

Raul is keeping a journal of his daily activities. Complete his sentences, using **yo** forms of each reflexive verb given. Remember, your answers must contain **two** words (a pronoun and a verb form) or it is not complete.

a. Yo _____ a las siete. (levantarse)

b. Yo _____ después. (ducharse)

c. Yo _____ la ropa. (ponerse)

d. Yo _____ del cereal. (desayunarse)

e. Yo _____ para la escuela. (irse)

f. Yo _____ a las diez. (acostarse)

g. Yo _____ pronto. (dormirse)

Ejercicio.

2.10

Each family member is very busy. They eat breakfast at different times. Express this, filling in the blanks with forms of the verb **desayunarse**.

a. El padre _____ a las seis.

b. La madre _____ a las ocho.

c. Paquito _____ a las siete y media.

d. Yo nunca _____ .

e. Mi hermano y yo nunca _____ .

f. Carmen _____ a las seis y cuarto.

g. El bebé _____ a las nueve.

h. Los domingos, la familia _____ después de la iglesia.

i. Los sábados mis hermanos _____ muy tarde.

j. Y tú. ¿Cuándo _____ ?

Ejercicio.

2.11

Fill in the blanks with a form of the given **reflexive** verbs:

a. Tú _____ muy temprano. (levantarse)

b. Ellos _____ del peso. (bajarse)

c. Nts. _____ a las nueve. (acostarse)

d. Yo _____ cuando estoy cansado. (irse)

e. Mariana _____ al restaurante. (almorzarse)

f. Los amigos _____ los dientes. (cepillarse)

g. Ud. y yo _____ en el espejo. (mirarse)

h. La madre de Elena _____ la chaqueta. (ponerse)

i. Uds. _____ muy elegante. (vestirse)

j. El _____ antes de dormirse. (banarse)

11

Compare the forms of each infinitive. Write the yo, nosotros, **and** tú **forms of each.**

2.12

	yo	nosotros	tú
a. Bañarse	_____	_____	_____
b. Irse	_____	_____	_____
c. ducharse	_____	_____	_____
d. ponerse	_____	_____	_____
e. dormirse	_____	_____	_____
f. aumentarse	_____	_____	_____
g. mirarse	_____	_____	_____
h. peinarse	_____	_____	_____
i. levantarse	_____	_____	_____
j. cenarse	_____	_____	_____

Translate the following sentences.

Translate numbers 1–5 from Spanish to English. Translate numbers 6–10 from English to Spanish.

2.13

1. Yo me baño por la manana.

2. Ellos se bajan de mucho peso.

3. Nts. Nos desayunamos a casa.

4. Concha se maquilla.

5. ¿Cuándo te duermes?

6. They gain weight.

7. You (formal) dress yourself well.

8. I take my clothes off before I take a shower.

9. After she washes the dog, she cleans (herself) off.

10. We look at ourselves in the mirror because we are going out tonight.

2.14   Write a ten-sentence paragraph describing what the people are doing in each of the above pictures.

_____

_____

_____

_____

_____

_____

_____

_____

_____

_____

_____

_____

Conversation Practice

> With a learning partner, create a conversation in Spanish using the suggestions given and present it to the class or to an adult.

2.15

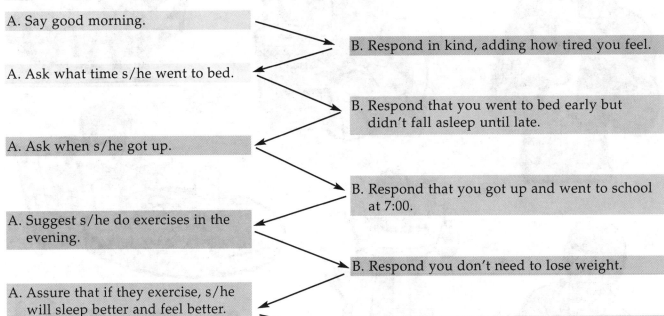

A. Say good morning.

B. Respond in kind, adding how tired you feel.

A. Ask what time s/he went to bed.

B. Respond that you went to bed early but didn't fall asleep until late.

A. Ask when s/he got up.

B. Respond that you got up and went to school at 7:00.

A. Suggest s/he do exercises in the evening.

B. Respond you don't need to lose weight.

A. Assure that if they exercise, s/he will sleep better and feel better.

B. Thank your friend.

✔ Adult check _____

Initial   Date

14

SELF TEST 2

2.01   **Fill in the blanks with the correct reflexive pronoun.** (3 pts. each)

a. (yo)_____ cepillo   (nts.) _____ cepillamos

b. (tú) _____ cepillas   (vts.) _____ cepilláis

c. (él) _____ cepilla   (ellos) _____ cepillan

d. (ella) _____ cepilla   (ellos) _____ cepillan

e. (Ud.) _____ cepilla   (Uds.) _____ cepillan

2.02   **Each sentence is missing one reflexive pronoun. Decide what that pronoun is and in which blank it belongs. Place a pronoun in only ONE blank.** (3 pts. each)

a. Por la mañana, a Carlitos le _____ gusta _____ lavar _____ el pelo.

b. No _____ puedo _____ bajar del peso facilmente.

c. _____ van _____ a las ocho?

d. Mis hermanas y yo no _____ maquillamos _____ . No nos gusta.

e. Tú vas _____ a _____ cepillar _____ los dientes.

2.03   **Write the form of the reflexive verb given.** (2 pts. each)

a. maquillarse (nts.)   _____

b. vestirse (yo)   _____

c. cepillarse (la nina)   _____

d. desayunarse (tú)   _____

e. ponerse (tú y yo)   _____

f. ponerse a dieta (los estudiantes)   _____

g. acostarse (Ud.)   _____

h. quitarse (Ricardo)   _____

i. banarse (mi madre)   _____

j. secarse (Uds.)   _____

2.04   **Rewrite the sentences, changing the reflexive verb form to agree with the new subject shown in parentheses. Hint: The *italicized* words are the words that need to be changed.** (5 pts. each)

a. Al *levantarnos, nos duchamos* y *nos cepillamos* los dientes. Entonces *nos desayunamos* y *nos vamos* a la escuela. (**la familia Rodriguez**)

b. *Yo me voy* al gran baile esa noche. Pero primero *tengo que ducharme*. Entonces, *me maquillo* y *me visto* del mejor traje. No *regreson* a casa y no *me acuesto* hasta las dos o las tres *por* manana. (**Tú**)

3. *Yo prefiero ducharme* por la noche. *Me cepillo* los dientes y *me acuesto por* las diez. Siempre me duermo pronto. Al amanecer, *me despierto* y *me levanto* bien. Despues de *desayunarme, me visto, me pongo,* una chaqueta y *me voy* al trabajo. (**Uds.**)

Score   _____

Teacher check   _____
                    Initial   Date

III. COMPREHENSION AND VOCABULARY: WEATHER CONDITIONS

Read the following passage and determine its meaning.

COMO PREPARARSE PARA LA ESCUELA

La primera cosa es dormirse bien. No se acuesta muy tarde, y se va a levantar temprano y descansado. Es buena idea decidir cómo va a vestirse para el día que viene a esa hora. Eso salva minutos mañana por la mañana. Siempre se desayuna de la comida nutriciosa. Come lentamente. Entonces se viste. Se pone la ropa propia para el tiempo. Si se pone la ropa correcta, no va a estar enfermo. Cuando se va para la escuela, es importante tener bastante tiempo. No te das prisa. El estrés de correr y preocuparse por la hora es malo para la salud. El secreto de prepararse bien para un día de éxito a la escuela es planear todo possible y ser organizado.

 Cuestiones para la comprensión.

3.1   a. ¿Es buena idea dormirse tarde?

b. ¿Cómo salva minutos por la manaña?

c. ¿Por qué debe ponerse la ropa apropriada para el tiempo?

d. ¿Cuál es una causa del estrés?

e. ¿Qué necesitas ser para tener un día de éxito a la escuela?

Write the Spanish for the weather and temperature, spelling out all numbers.

3.2

a.

_____

_____

b.

_____

_____

c.

_____

_____

d.

_____

_____

e.

_____

_____

f.

_____

_____

g.

_____

_____

h.
_____
_____

i.
_____
_____

j.
_____
_____

For each of the seasons listed below, write in Spanish two typical weather conditions and the average temperature. Please use a region where there are definite weather changes.

3.3

a. la primavera_____

_____

b. el invierno_____

_____

c. el otoño_____

_____

d. el verano _____

_____

SELF TEST 3

3.01   **Label the pictures with the weather expression that is depicted.** (4 pts. each)

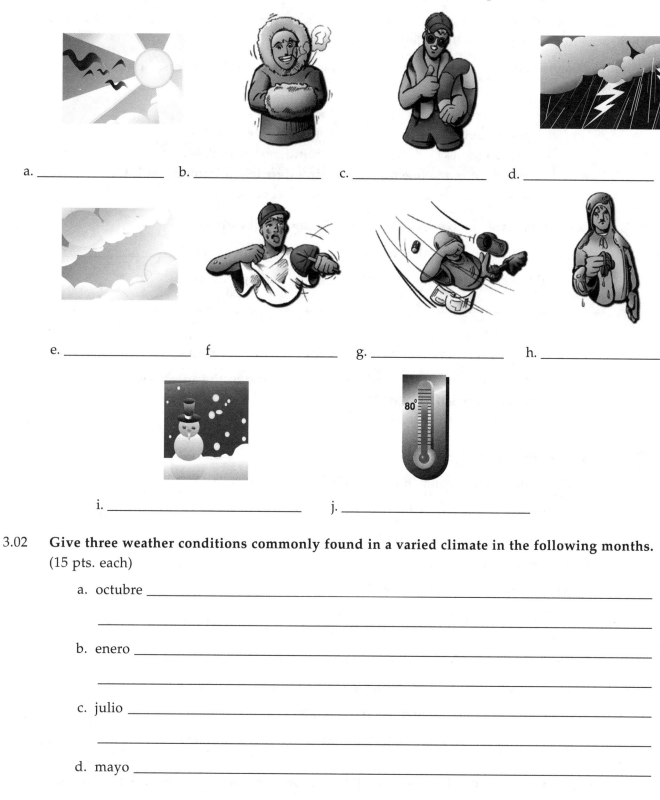

a. _____   b. _____   c. _____   d. _____

e. _____   f. _____   g. _____   h. _____

i. _____   j. _____

3.02   **Give three weather conditions commonly found in a varied climate in the following months.**
(15 pts. each)

a. octubre _____

_____

b. enero _____

_____

c. julio _____

_____

d. mayo _____

_____

Score   _____

Teacher check _____
                   Initial   Date

IV. GRAMMAR: ADVERBS AND DEMONSTRATIVE ADJECTIVES

Adverbs

An adverb is a word that describes how an action is performed; that is, how something is done. In English, adverbs usually end with the letters "-ly."

As most English adverbs feature a special ending, so do Spanish adverbs. Compare the following adjectives and their corresponding adverbs:

lento (slow)	**lentamente** (slowly)
rápido (quick)	**rápidamente** (quickly)
inteligente (intelligent)	**inteligentement** (intelligently)

 Refer to the table above and answer the following questions.

4.1   What was added to each adjective in order to make it an adverb? _____

4.2   How did the adjective change before adding the ending **-mente**?

_____

Therefore, the rule for forming a Spanish adverb is:

1. **Choose the FEMININE SINGULAR form of the adjective.**
2. **Add the suffix "-MENTE"**

 Answer the following questions.

4.3   If **frío** is Spanish for "cold," how would you phrase "coldly?"

a. What is the feminine of **frio**? _____

b. Now add on the adverbial suffix: _____

4.4   Do the same for **perfecto**.

a. What is the feminine of **perfecto**? _____

b. Now add on the adverbial suffix: _____

 Refer to the first table above and answer the following questions.

4.5   Why didn't **inteligente** seem to change its spelling before adding the suffix?

a. Does the adjective **inteligente** have a gender? _____

b. Does **inteligente** change spelling for masculine and feminine nouns? _____

Therefore, neutral adjectives will NOT change spelling for the formation of adverbs.

The English adverbs for "good" and "bad" are "well" and "poorly." In Spanish they are as follows:

bueno – bien

malo – mal

22

Change the following adjectives to the feminine forms in the first blank then change those feminine adjectives to adverbs.

4.6　　a. enojado　　　＿＿＿＿＿＿＿＿＿＿＿＿＿＿　＿＿＿＿＿＿＿＿＿＿＿＿＿＿

　　　　b. bonitos　　　＿＿＿＿＿＿＿＿＿＿＿＿＿＿　＿＿＿＿＿＿＿＿＿＿＿＿＿＿

　　　　c. alto　　　　＿＿＿＿＿＿＿＿＿＿＿＿＿＿　＿＿＿＿＿＿＿＿＿＿＿＿＿＿

　　　　d. cuidadoso　　＿＿＿＿＿＿＿＿＿＿＿＿＿＿　＿＿＿＿＿＿＿＿＿＿＿＿＿＿

　　　　e. decente　　　＿＿＿＿＿＿＿＿＿＿＿＿＿＿　＿＿＿＿＿＿＿＿＿＿＿＿＿＿

　　　　f. propio　　　＿＿＿＿＿＿＿＿＿＿＿＿＿＿　＿＿＿＿＿＿＿＿＿＿＿＿＿＿

　　　　g. solo　　　　＿＿＿＿＿＿＿＿＿＿＿＿＿＿　＿＿＿＿＿＿＿＿＿＿＿＿＿＿

　　　　h. insonorosos　＿＿＿＿＿＿＿＿＿＿＿＿＿＿　＿＿＿＿＿＿＿＿＿＿＿＿＿＿

　　　　i. permanente　＿＿＿＿＿＿＿＿＿＿＿＿＿＿　＿＿＿＿＿＿＿＿＿＿＿＿＿＿

　　　　j. raros　　　　＿＿＿＿＿＿＿＿＿＿＿＿＿＿　＿＿＿＿＿＿＿＿＿＿＿＿＿＿

Spanish adverbs are used within sentences in the same manner their English counterparts are.

 Identify the adjective in each sentence by underlining it. Next, complete the following sentence by changing that adjective into an adverb. Complete the translation also.

4.7　　a. Alberto está furioso.　　　Alberto habla＿＿＿＿＿＿＿＿＿＿＿＿＿＿＿＿＿＿

　　　　　Al is furious.　　　　　Albert speaks＿＿＿＿＿＿＿＿＿＿＿＿＿＿＿＿＿

　　　　b. Yo estoy emocionada.　　　Yo me muevo＿＿＿＿＿＿＿＿＿＿＿＿＿＿＿＿＿

　　　　　I am excited.　　　　　I move＿＿＿＿＿＿＿＿＿＿＿＿＿＿＿＿＿＿＿＿

　　　　c. Uds. son inteliegentes.　　Uds. Escriben＿＿＿＿＿＿＿＿＿＿＿＿＿＿＿＿＿

　　　　　You are intelligent.　　　You write＿＿＿＿＿＿＿＿＿＿＿＿＿＿＿＿＿＿

　　　　d. Nts. Estamos correctos.　　Nosotros nos portamos＿＿＿＿＿＿＿＿＿＿＿＿

　　　　　We are correct.　　　　We behave ourselves ＿＿＿＿＿＿＿＿＿＿＿＿＿

　　　　e. Tú eres cortés.　　　　Hablas＿＿＿＿＿＿＿＿＿＿＿＿＿＿＿＿＿＿＿＿＿

　　　　　You are courteous.　　　You speak ＿＿＿＿＿＿＿＿＿＿＿＿＿＿＿＿＿＿

Demonstrative Adjectives

In English, demonstrative adjectives are the words **this**, **that**, **those** and **these**. They point out, or demonstrate, a particular noun within a group. For example, when making a choice you may be asked, "Which coat do you want?" You may answer, "I want that green coat." The demonstrative adjective differentiates the one green coat from the others.

Here are the Spanish demonstrative adjectives.

THIS/THESE	THAT/THOSE (close by the speaker)	THAT/THOSE (far from the speaker)
este	ese	aquel
esta	esa	aquella
estos	esos	aquellos
estas	esas	aquellas

Why are there so many for each? Demonstratives are adjectives, and like all Spanish adjectives they must agree in number and gender with their nouns.

Translate the the following sentences.

4.8   a. Miro este programa. _____

b. Miro ese programa._____

c. Miro aquel programa. _____

d. Quiero estas galletas._____

e. Quiero esas galletas. _____

f. Quiero aquellas galletas. _____

SPANISH

O N E

LIFEPAC 7
TEST

80 / 100

Name _____

Date _____

Score _____

SPANISH I: LIFEPAC TEST 7

1. Make the following verbs reflexive by adding the agreeing reflexive pronoun. (1 pt. each)

   a. _____ baño

   b. _____ sientan

   c. _____ despide

   d. _____ marchas

   e. _____ quitamos

   f. _____ escriben

   g. _____ despierto

   h. _____ ve

   i. _____ conoces

   j. _____ pone

2. Complete the verb list by filling in the blanks with the correct form of the given reflexive verbs. (1 pt. each)

   a. cepillarse (tú) _____

   b. maquillarse (yo) _____

   c. sentarse (nts.) _____

   d. irse (Usted) _____

   e. vestirse (Ellas) _____

   f. mirarse (los niños) _____

   g. ducharse (Elena) _____

   h. acercarse (tú y yo) _____

   i. encontrarse (Uds.) _____

   j. prepararse (mi mamá) _____

3. Choose from the list of adjectives below to complete the translations of adverbs. Remember to add the appropriate suffix. (1 pt. each)

corto	rico
pesado	aburrido
inteligente	estúpido
natural	preferible
posible	raro

1

a. rarely _____

b. heavily _____

c. richly _____

d. naturally _____

e. stupidly _____

f. preferably _____

g. boringly _____

h. smartly _____

i. possibly _____

j. shortly _____

4. Change the given demonstrative pronoun to the one indicated. (1 pt. each)

a. aquella gata   (this)   _____ gata

b. estos vasos   (those /close)   _____ vasos

c. esta mujer   (that / far)   _____ mujer

d. esa computadora   (this)   _____ computadora

e. aquellos amigos   (these)   _____ amigos

f. ese coche   (that / far)   _____ coche

g. estas clases   (that /close)   _____ clases

h. aquellos hombres   (these)   _____ hombres

i. estas plumas   (those /close)   _____ plumas

j. esas líneas   (these)   _____ líneas

5. Translate the weather phrases. (3 pts. each)

a. It's sunny. _____

b. It's raining. _____

c. It's hot. _____

d. It's snowing. _____

e. It's cool. _____

f. It's cold. _____

g. It's 98 degrees. _____

h. The weather is good. _____

i. It's 12 degrees. _____

j. The weather is bad. _____

6. Answer the following questions in complete sentences. (6 pts. each)

    a. ¿Qué tiempo hace en otoño?

    b. ¿Quién corre rápidamente?

    c. ¿De quién es esta casa?

    d. ¿Por qué lees este libro?

    e. ¿A qué hora te despiertas por la mañana?

It is also important to understand the multiple functions these words carry for the Spanish language. Not only do they carry the meanings "this, that, these or those," they also reflect number and gender AND indicate physical position relative to the speaker. Both of the sentences below translate as "I can see that boat."

Here is the difference: By using the word **ese** in the first sentence, we know the boat is physically close to the speaker. By using the word **aquel** in the second, we know the boat is off in the distance, physically far from the speaker.

Note: The definite and indefinite articles are not necessary when using demonstrative adjectives. In English, the phrases "right here" or "over here" replaces the **ese** group. The **aquel** group is replaced with the phrase "over there" in order to indicate physical proximity.

 For each group of nouns, change the given demonstrative adjective to agree in number and gender.

4.9   a. **ese**   _____ niño

                           _____ coches

                           _____ mujeres

                           _____ chica

        b. **aquella** _____ lápiz

                           _____ banderas

                           _____ hombres

                           _____ hermana

        d. **estos**   _____ tareas

                           _____ clase

                           _____ objetos

                           _____ chaleco

25

Fill in the blanks with the correct form of the demonstrative adjective indicated in parentheses.

4.10　　a. Necesito_____ cuaderno. (that, close by)

b. Me gusta _____ perro. (this)

c. Quieres_____ sombrero. (this)

d. Prefiere_____ computadora. (that, far away)

e. Nos gusta _____ edificios. (these)

f. Leo_____ revista. (that, close by)

g. Pasas_____ casas. (those, far away)

h. Requiero _____ novelas. (these)

i. Compran_____ bicicletas. (those, close by)

j. Bailamos con_____ chica. (that, far away)

With a learning partner create a conversation in Spanish, using the suggestions given, and present it to the class or to an adult.

4.11

A. Greet your friend, adding what beautiful weather you're having

B. Respond in kind with a greeting. Ask if s/he is well.

A. Respond yes. Ask if this is a new jacket s/he is wearing.

B. Respond no, that this is an old jacket your brother generously gave (dio) you.

A. Ask if you know that new girl at school

B. Respond by pointing; does s/he mean that girl (over there)? She dresses elegantly.

A. Respond yes. Add that she speaks Spanish wonderfully.

B. Respond no, but you intend to meet her as quickly as possible.

A. Offer to say hello together during lunch.

B. Respond OK, until then.

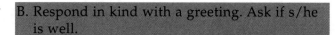

✔ Adult check _____

Initial　　　　　　　　　　　Date

SELF TEST 4

4.01   **Change the given adjectives to adverbs.** (4 pts. each)

   a. gracioso – thankful: _____ – thankfully

   b. bonita – beautiful: _____ – beautifully

   c. cierto – certain: _____ – certainly

   d. alto – high: _____ – highly

   e. perfecto – perfect: _____ – perfectly

   f. malo – bad: _____ – badly

   g. estricto – strict: _____ – strictly

   h. raro – rare: _____ – rarely

   i. bueno – good: _____ – well

   j. triste – sad: _____ – sadly

   k. entero – entire: _____ – entirely

   Imagine a couple is driving in an unfamiliar town. One tries to give instructions, but the driver just can't seem to get them straight. Fill in their dialogue, using demonstrative adjectives and the clues provided. (3 pts. each)

4.02   a. Mira, dobla a la derecha a _____ avenida. (this)

   b. ¿ _____ avenida? (that/far away)

   a. ¡Ay! ¡No, no! ¡ _____ avenida! (that/close)

4.03   a. Bueno, pasa _____ edificio. (that/far away)

   b. Dices, ¿ _____ edificio? (this)

   a. ¡No, no! ¡ _____ edificio! (that/close)

4.04   a. ¿Por qué doblas a _____ señales(f) (these)

   b. ¿No me dices que doble a _____ señales? (those/far away)

   a. ¡Nunca me eschuchas! ¡ Dobla a _____ señales! (those/close)

4.05   a. Cuidado, hay un policía a _____ esquina. (that/close)

   b. ¿ _____ esquina? (that/far away)

   a. ¡No, no! ¡ _____ esquina! (this)

4.06   a. Por fin. ¡ _____ hoteles son de mi padre! (those/near)

   b. ¿ _____ hoteles? (these)

   a. ¡ _____ hoteles! ¡ _____ hoteles! (those/far away)

74 / 92	

Score   _____

Teacher check   _____
                   Initial   Date

27

V. NATIVE CULTURES OF CENTRAL & SOUTH AMERICA

THE AZTECS

The **Aztec Indians** maintained a huge, powerful empire covering most of what is today the country of Mexico. When the Spanish conquerors reached their capital city of **Tenochtitlan**, they were amazed at the civilization built essentially in a swamp. The Aztecs were skilled architects, builders and craftsmen. Their civilization was noted for its extensive systems of canals, aqueducts and bridges which were needed to survive and travel through the once marshy terrain. Tenochtitlan was constructed mainly of artificial islands, called **chinamapas**.

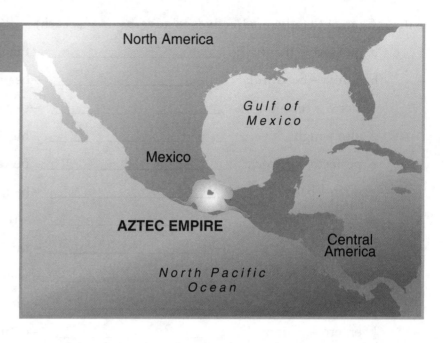

The Aztecs were also known for their development of a highly accurate calendar, pictographic writing, called **codices** and their understanding of the mathematical concept of zero. These are still considered outstanding accomplishments for what was once regarded as a "primitive" society.

Aztec folklore was based largely on a number of nature gods and was warrior-like and violent. To die in battle serving the empire was a great honor. Ritual human sacrifice was necessary to placate their gods.

Aztec folklore traces the origins of the empire to a deserted marshland. Within that swamp a priest came upon a cactus growing from a rock on which was perched an eagle eating a snake. It was at this site the city of Tenochtitlan was built. The national symbol of Mexico is still the eagle and the snake, and can be seen on the Mexican flag, a passing nod to the Aztec heritage of the nation.

Aztec Calendar

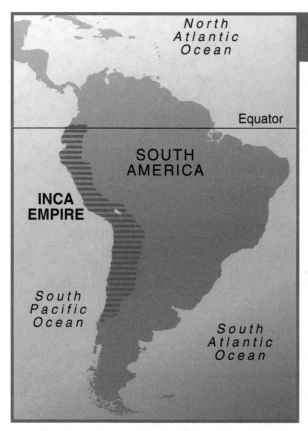

The empire of the **Incas**, centered mainly in the Andean region of Peru, is chiefly known today for having maintained the most highly advanced society of all the native cultures.

The Incas were a highly political society. The government is best described as an agricultural theocracy; that is, a divinely chosen king ruled over a society powered economically by farming. Like the Aztecs, the Incas formed a classed society. Beneath the royal family came artisans, then laborers (non-land owning peoples). The government carefully supervised and regulated the selection and planting of crops. A portion of every citizen's crops was handed over to the royal family as a form of taxes. Surprisingly, the Inca government also educated the laborers in the ways of horticulture, thus ensuring its own (and the empire's) long life.

The Incas were known also as astronomers, road builders and engineers. They constructed amazing rope suspension bridges. They also developed a numerical system of record-keeping in order to keep track of tax collection and for recording crop yield—all without the assistance of the wheel. It is interesting to note that a society which had never achieved use of the wheel had developed written language; today that language is called **Quechua**.

The Incas looked to the heavens and the earth for religious inspiration. They were highly interested in astronomy, looking to heavenly gods to choose their leaders and natural gods for guidance running their daily lives. Animal sacrifice was routinely practiced.

Machu Picchu

In the end, Pizarro conquered the Inca people. Largely assimilated into the Spanish culture, their most enduring mark is the enigmatic **Machu Picchu**. Machu Picchu was the Andean home of the Incas. Strangely abandoned long before Pizarro, it remained undiscovered for centuries high up in the Andes Mountains. Today anthropologists still have no explanation for the mysterious disappearance of its peoples. The greatest threat to Machu Picchu today is the eroding effects of heavy rainfall from tropical storms.

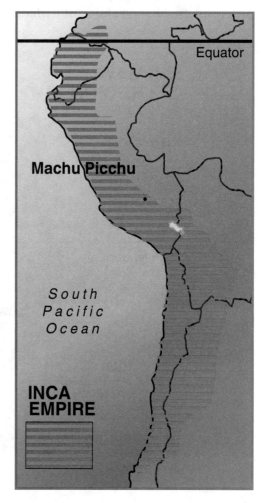

THE MAYA

The **Maya** Indians are still with us today, living primarily in Mexico, Guatemala, Belize and Honduras. Their native language, **Yucatec**, is still spoken in modern times.

Like other native American cultures, the Maya formed an agrarian society. Their chief products were corn and the cacao bean (from which chocolate is derived). Neither of these products existed in Europe until the conquest of these peoples by the Spanish.

MAYA REGION

Gulf of Mexico

North Pacific Ocean

Central America

The ancient Mayan culture is, interestingly, full of contradictions. While the Maya had domesticated dogs, they had not achieved the management of large work animals like the Incas did. They were expert metal workers. Their expertise, however, did not extend beyond ornamental workings of gold and copper. They had no metal tools or weapons and had not yet achieved use of the wheel. This proved to aid their own destruction by the Spanish, as the Mayans could not compete in war against armed soldiers on horseback.

In our times the Maya are remembered for their stunning achievements in architecture, writing and calendar systems. The pyramids of **Chichén Itzá** and **Palenque**, used primarily as centers of religious devotion, rival those of Egypt. They developed an extensive system of hieroglyphic writing, maintained in collections called **codices**, or **codex**.

MAYA REGION

Gulf of Mexico

Chichén Itzá

YUCATÁN MAYA

Palenque

Caribbean Sea

LOWLANDS MAYA

GUATEMALAN HIGHLANDS MAYA

North Pacific Ocean

Chichén Itzá

Palenque

SELF TEST 5

5.01 **Decide which tribe is being discussed. Write the names** Aztec, Maya **or** Inca **in the blanks, as needed.** (2 pts. each)

a. _____ Metal workers, mostly for ornamentation

b. _____ Used aqueducts and bridges to navigate swampy terrain

c. _____ Capital city of Tenochtitlan

d. _____ Agriculturally-centered government

e. _____ Empire spread over Mexico and Central America

f. _____ Written language (Quechua)

g. _____ Developed highly accurate calendar

h. _____ Peruvian, lived in Andes mountains

i. _____ Native language, Yucatec, still spoken today

j. _____ Empire covered Mexico

5.02 **Verdadero o Falso. Write** V **or** F **in the blank.** (2 pts. each)

a. _____ The Maya are known to have developed a highly accurate calendar.

b. _____ Macchu Picchu was built by the Maya.

c. _____ The capital city of the Aztec empire was called Tenochtitlan.

d. _____ The Maya had achieved use of the wheel.

e. _____ The Aztec natives were located primarily in what is known today as Mexico.

f. _____ The Inca civilization "disappeared," and its loss is largely a mystery today.

g. _____ The Inca system of writing was maintained in the **codex** books.

h. _____ The native language of the Maya is called **Yucatec**.

i. _____ The eagle and the snake are symbols of the Inca empire.

j. _____ The Inca empire was located primarily in what is known today as Peru.

5.03 **On the lines provided below, correct the five false statements found in question 5.02.** (4 pts. each)

a. _____

b. _____

c. _____

d. _____

e. _____

5.04 **Fill in the blanks to accurately complete the sentences.** (3 pts. each answer)

a. The Inca city of Macchu Picchu is located high in the _____ mountains.

b. The Aztecs are also known for understanding the concept of the number _____ .

c. The Inca language is called _____ .

d. The _____ of the Mayan civilization rival those of Egypt.

e. The _____ and the _____ are still national symbols of Mexico and are found on the flag today.

f. An agricultural society which is ruled by a divinely chosen king is called an

_____ _____ .

g. The Inca empire was centered mainly in the region of _____ .

h. The Aztec empire was centered mainly in the region of _____ .

i. The effects of heavy _____ are the greatest threat to Macchu Picchu.

j. Chocolate is derived from the _____ bean.

VI. REVIEW EXERCISES

Write the letter of the verb form that agrees with the subject given in each sentence.

6.1

1. La familia _____ a amigos los sábados.
   a. dan   b. da   c. dáis

2. Marcos _____ un documental por la televisión.
   a. veo   b. ven   c. ve

3. Yo _____ a la iglesia.
   a. doy   b. dáis   c. damos

4. Tú _____ conmigo a la fiesta.
   a. viene   b. vienen   c. vienes

5. Nosotros _____ a las cinco en punto.
   a. vamos   b. váis   c. voy

6. Ustedes _____ mucho que estudiar.
   a. tiene   b. tengo   c. tienen

7. Elena y yo _____ las gracias a la profesora.
   a. da   b. doy   c. damos

8. Rico y Usted _____ una casa a lo lejos.
   a. ven   b. ve   c. véis

9. Usted y Usted _____ a la biblioteca el viernes
   a. van   b. vamos   c. va

10. ¿Qué _____ yo en mi bolsillo?
    a. tenemos   b. tenéis   c. tengo

11. Yo voy a _____ una sorpresa a tí.
    a. doy   b. dan   c. dar

12. ¿No te _____ en el espejo?
    a. ves   b. ver   c. ve

13. La clase _____ al museo temprano.
    a. vienes   b. vienen   c. viene

14. ¿Quiénes _____ conmigo?
    a. vamos   b. van   c. vas

15. La madre de mi _____ mucho que hacer.
    a. tengo   b. tiene   c. tener

Write the letter of the answer that correctly completes the math problem.

6.2

1. **nueve + uno = _____ .**
   a. quince   b. diez   c. viente

2. **diez y ocho – cuatro = _____ .**
   a. once   b. cuatro   c. catorce

3. **quince x dos = _____ .**
   a. trece   b. treinta   c. tres

4. **trienta + cuarenta = _____ .**
   a. ochenta   b. sesenta   c. setenta

5. **diez y siete + treinta y tres = _____ .**
   a. cincuenta   b. vienta y siete   c. noventa

6. **nueve x cinco = _____ .**
   a. doce   b. dos   c. cuarenta y cinco

7. **trece + cuarenta y cuatro = _____ .**
   a. diez y siete   b. cuarenta y siete   c. viente y siete

8. **viente y cinco x dos = _____ .**
   a. cien   b. cincuenta   c. cero

9. **once + viente y uno = _____ .**
   a. seis   b. noventa y cinco   c. treinta y dos

10. **ochenta y cinco – setenta y uno = _____ .**
    a. sesenta y nueve   b. catorce   c. cien

Fill in the blanks with the correct Spanish number.

6.3

a. diez y ocho – quince = _____ .

b. cuarenta y dos – _____ = doce.

c. _____ – veinte y seis = veinte y tres.

d. Cien – _____ = diez y siete.

e. Treinta + _____ = cuarenta y uno

f. Noventa y uno – _____ = cincuenta.

g. Sesenta y siete + _____ = setenta y siete

h. _____ + cincuenta = cincuenta.

i. Catorce – _____ = uno.

j. Veinte y ocho – diez y siete = _____ .

Write the letter of the matching fruit or vegetable.

1. _____ una cebolla

2. _____ los guisantes

3. _____ la pera

4. _____ la lechuga

5. _____ la naranja

6. _____ el plátano

7. _____ los tomates

8. _____ las zanahorias

9. _____ la manzana

10. _____ la piña

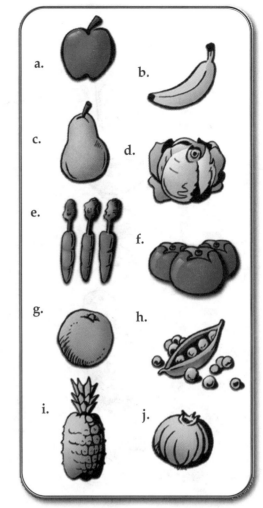

Match the vocabulary to the pictures.

1. _____ la sopa

2. _____ el carne asada

3. _____ el jamón

4. _____ el pescado

5. _____ una hamburguesa

6. _____ el pollo

7. _____ una ensalada

8. _____ el biftec

9. _____ el arroz

10. _____ el sánwich

a.

b.

c.

d.

e.

f.

g.

h.

i.

j.

If the sentence correctly identifies the picture, write verdadero **in the space provided. If not, write** falso *and* **the correct Spanish term next to it.**

6.6   1.   ¿Es el agua?   _____ : _____

        2.   ¿Es el panqueque?   _____ : _____

        3.   ¿Es la torta?   _____ : _____

        4.   ¿Es el jugo?   _____ : _____

        5.   ¿Es la tarta?   _____ : _____

        6.   ¿Es el café?   _____ : _____

        7.   ¿Es el helado?   _____ : _____

        8.   ¿Es la tortilla?   _____ : _____

        9.   ¿Es el papa?   _____ : _____

        10.   ¿Es la leche?   _____ : _____

Expressions With TENER

Match each situation below with a correct expression of tener **found in the list below. Make sure to use the correct form of** tener **in your answer.**

tener sed	tener prisa	tener miedo
tener ganas de	tener hambre	tener calor
tener frío	tener sueno	tener suerte
tener razón	no tener razon	

6.7

a. Yo necesito el agua: Yo _____ .

b. Es diciembre. Ellos _____ .

c. Nts. Ganamos mucho dinero. Nts. _____ .

d. El ve una película de horror. El _____ .

e. Tú no comes mucho. Tu no _____ .

f. Ellas están tarde. Ellas _____ .

g. Es medianoche. Ud. _____ .

h. Quieren bailar. Uds. _____ ir a la discoteca.

i. ¿2 + 2 = 5? Yo _____ .

j. Necesito un vaso de agua. Yo _____ .

Here is a list of ten sentences using expressions of tener. **Rewrite each, changing what is necessary to complete the translations.**

6.8

a. Tú tienes hambre.

I am hungry: _____ .

b. Maria tiene prisa.

Maria is afraid:_____ .

c. Tú y yo tenemos ganas de salir.

We don't feel like reading: _____ .

d. Usted tiene sed.

They are thirsty:_____ .

e. Tú tienes calor.

All of you are warm: _____ .

f. Enrique tiene razón.

I am right:_____ .

g. La Srta. tiene suerte.

We are lucky: _____ .

h. La clase tiene prisa.

I am in a hurry: _____ .

i. Yo tengo ganas de comer las hamburguesas.

All of you feel like studying: _____ .

j. Tú tienes razón.

You are sleepy: _____ .

Here are five situations. Write how you feel in each situation, using an expression of tener. Be logical.

6.9   a. Es enero, y la temperatura es cinco grados.

b. La clase es a las nueve de la mañana. Ya son las nueve y quince.

c. Crees que la cuidad de los Estados Unidos es Montana.

d. Necesito una bebida y no hay ningúna agua.

e. Estudias mucho en casa y son las once de la noche.

GUSTAR

Fill in the blanks with the proper form of gustar **or pronoun found in the list below. Some anwers will be used more than once.**

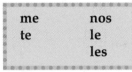

me	nos
te	le
	les

6.10   a. A mí _____ gusta comer al aire libre. ¿Y a tí, _____ gusta?

   b. No, me _____ los restaurantes mejor. Voy con Arturo y a él

   _____ mejor tambien.

   c. Cuando vamos a la playa nos _____ broncearnos. A nosotros

   _____ gusta usar la crema bronceadora.

   d. A mi familia le _____ jugar al futbol.

   e. A Uds. _____ gusta el hockey.

   f. ¿Qué te _____ hacer los sábados?

   g. A Ricardo y yo _____ _____ estudiar en silencio.

   h. No me _____ los exámenes.

   i. Prefiere escuchar la radio. _____ gusta el ruido bajo.

   j. ¿No necesitas la ropa nueva? ¿ _____ gusta ir de compras conmigo?

IR Idioms

The sentences below describe what the person is doing *now.* **Change them, using a form of** Ir + A + infinitive, **to discuss what they are** *going* **to do tomorrow. Follow the model.**

Yo camino por el parque: Yo voy a caminar por el parqe.

6.11   a. Ramon escribe una tarea:_____ .

   b. Nts. Vamos a una fiesta:_____ .

   c. Pido un helado en un restaurante: _____ .

   d. Aprendes montar una bicicleta: _____ .

   e. Ustedes compran la ropa nueva: _____ .

   f. Viajo a la casa de mi abuelita: _____ .

   g. Usted ayuda a su mamá: _____ .

   h. Los estudiantes están de vacaciones: _____ .

   i. La clase sufre un examen: _____ .

   j. Me baño: _____ .

Answer the following questions in complete Spanish sentences, using a form of IR + A + infinitive.

6.12   1. ¿Cómo vas a viajar a la escuela?

2. ¿Qué vas a comer para el desayuno?

3. ¿Quién va a llamar por teléfono a Usted?

4. ¿Cuándo vas a graduarte del colegio?

5. ¿Dónde vas a estudiar?

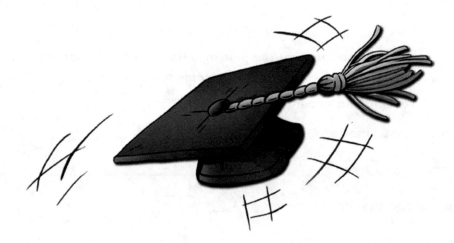

Note: This section does not have a Self Test.

VII. VOCABULARY DRILL

 For each illustration below, circle the Spanish vocabulary word that correctly identifies the activity.

7.1   a. mirarse / secarse   b. lavarse / ponerse   c. despertarse / acostarse

d. ponerse a dieta / ducharse   e. quitarse / maquillarse   f. bañarse / secarse

g. pasearse / ponerse   h. dormirse / levantarse   i. vestirse / quitarse

j. irse / aumentarse de peso   k. bañarse / ducharse   l. vestirse / cepillarse

41

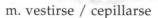
m. vestirse / cepillarse

n. despertarse / levantarse

o. irse / bajarse de peso

 Matching.

7.2

_____ 1. El jabón		a. the shoes
_____ 2. El dormitorio		b. the mirror
_____ 3. La secadora del pelo		c. the toothbrush
_____ 4. La bañera		d. the soap
_____ 5. Los zapatos		e. the breakfast
_____ 6. El espejo		f. the dinner, supper
_____ 7. El cepillo para dientes		g. the bedroom
_____ 8. El desayuno		h. the bathtub
_____ 9. La toalla		i. the hair dryer
_____10. La cena		j. the towel

Weather Conditions

For each month given, list *two* logical weather conditions. First, state the actual weather phenomena. On the second line, state the average temperature. Write out all numbers. Try to use the most common conditions associated with that time of the year.

7.3

a. diciembre: _____

_____

b. agosto:_____

_____

c. octubre:_____

_____

d. abril:_____

_____

e. marzo:_____

_____

Reflexive Verb Forms

Fill in the blanks with the correct reflexive pronouns.

cortarse – to cut oneself

7.4

a. _____ corto   d. _____ cortamos

b. _____ cortas   e. _____ cortáis

c. _____ corta   f. _____ cortan

Choose the correct verb form.

7.5

1. Por la mañana, yo _____ a las seis.

   a. te bañas   b. se baña   c. me baño

2. Te gusta _____ temprano.

   a. te acuestas   b. acostarte   c. acostarme

3. Ella siempre _____ en el espejo antes de salir.

   a. se mira   b. se miran   c. nos miramos

4. Ustedes _____ enfrente del espejo.

   a. se maquilla   b. maquillarse   c. se maquillan

5. Tú y yo _____ los abrigos cuando hace frío.

   a. ponerse   b. ponernos   c. nos ponemos

6. Mariana _____ de la tienda a las nueve en punto.

   a. se va   b. se van   c. irte

7. La clase _____ al restaurante mexicano.

   a. se pasean   b. se pasea   c. nos paseamos

8. El y sus hermanos prefieren _____ muy tarde.

   a. se acuesta   b. acostarse   c. se acuestan

9. Usted _____ en vez de banarse.

   a. se ducha   b. ducharse   c. se duchan

10. Yo necesito _____ el pelo con la secadora.

    a. me seco   b. te secas   c. secarme

Write the forms of the given reflexive infinitives. Each answer should have *two* words: a reflexive pronoun and an agreeing verb form.

7.6   a. bañarse (nts.)   _____

b. desayunarse (tu)   _____

c. acostarse (ellos)   _____

d. cepillarse (Usted)   _____

e. lavarse (yo)   _____

f. secarse (el hijo)   _____

g. quitarse (Ud. y Ud.)   _____

h. peinarse (tu y yo)   _____

i. ponerse (Ricardo)   _____

j. irse (tu)   _____

k. maquillarse (las chicas) _____

l. ducharse (nts)   _____

m. vestirse (mis amigos)   _____

n. dormirse (la estudiante) _____

o. despertarse (el)   _____

Fill in the agreeing reflexive pronoun in the appropriate blank. One or two spaces in each problem will be left blank.

7.7   a. Ella está enojada y _____ va _____ rapidamente.

b. Yo _____ despierto _____ temprano.

c. Ella no va a _____ duchar _____ hasta la manana.

d. _____ prefieren _____ vestir bien.

e. Despues de trabajar en el jardin, tú _____ lavas _____ en el baño.

f. ¡Ay cuánto que comí! Yo voy _____ a _____ aumentar _____ de peso.

g. ¡ _____ no _____ levanta _____ ella a tiempo?

h. Nunca sale sin _____ maquillar _____ .

i. Necesito una toalla. Yo _____ seco _____ pronto.

j. Hace frío. Uds. _____ ponen _____ un abrigo.

Adverbs

What adjective did these adverbs come from? Drop the adverbial ending and write the orginal Spanish adjective in the blank.

7.8
    a. elegantemente: _____

    b. cruelmente: _____

    c. antipaticamente: _____

    d. celosamente: _____

    e. armargamente: _____

    f. inteligentemente: _____

    g. interesadamente: _____

    h. lujosamente: _____

    i. encantadamente: _____

    j. dificilmente: _____

Change these adjectives into adverbs.

7.9
    a. alta: _____

    b. rico: _____

    c. bonito: _____

    d. pesada: _____

    e. aburrido: _____

    f. malo: _____

    g. cariñoso: _____

    h. fácil: _____

    i. hábil: _____

    j. satisfecho: _____

Demonstrative Adjectives

Choose the demonstrative adjective that agrees in number and gender.

7.10

1. Prefiero comer en _____ restaurante.

   a. este   b. esta   c. estos

2. Compramos _____ coche.

   a. aquella   b. aquellos   c. aquel

3. ¡ _____ regalo es para mi!

   a. Ese   b. Esa   c. Esas

4. Quiere diez dólares por _____ ventana rota.

   a. esa   b. esas   c. esos

5. ¿No puedes ver _____ edificio?

   a. aquella   b. aquellos   c. aquel

6. Marca la tarea con _____ bolígrafo.

   a. esta   b. este   c. estos

7. Recibio _____ sueter para su cumpleaños.

   a. ese   b. esos   c. esa

8. Me seco con _____ toalla.

   a. aquella   b. aquel   c. aquellas

9. Nos gustan _____ ropas.

   a. estos   b. esta   c. estas

10. Ella está leyendo _____ libro.

    a. aquella   b. aquellos   c. aquel

In order to complete the translations, fill in the blanks with a correct, agreeing demonstrative adjective chosen from the list below. Some will be used more than once.

este	ese	aquel
esta	esa	aquella
estos	esos	aquellos
estas	esas	aquellas

7.11

a. I need that hat!   ¡Necesito _____ sombrero!

b. Give me that (far) flower.   Dáme _____ flor (f.s.).

c. He ate those apples.   El comió _____ manzanas.

d. She wants this soap? ¿Quiere _____ jabon?

e. We used that (far) house. Usamos _____ casa.

f. You drive those cars. Conduce _____ automoviles.

g. She takes those medicines. Ella toma _____ medicinas.

h. I made those (far) chairs. Hice _____ sillas.

i. This film is awful. ¡ _____ película es horrible!

j. These salads are delicious. _____ ensaladas son deliciosas.

Translate the phrases. Use the vocabulary found at the end of this LIFEPAC. Be sure to use a demonstrative adjective in each answer.

7.12   a. that (close) mirror _____

b. these toothbrushes _____

c. this bedroom _____

d. those bathtubs _____

e. that (far) clock _____

f. those (near) shoes _____

g. these combs _____

h. that (near) brush _____

i. that (far) bathroom _____

j. this toothpaste _____

k. these hair dryers _____

l. that (near) towel _____

m. those (far) showers _____

n. this shampoo _____

o. those (near) lunches _____

Reading Comprehension

 Read the following passage. Try to follow the general story line. It is not necessary to translate every single word.

Maria:	¿Puedo desayunarme contigo, Ramona?
Ramona:	Sí, Sí, conozco un buen restaurante. Es muy elegante.
Maria:	¿Se viste bien en aquel restaurante?
Ramona:	Sí, muy finamente. Te pones un traje.
Maria:	¿Un traje? ¿No son buenos estos jeans y esta camiseta?
Ramona:	No, esas ropas no son buenas. ¡No se viste casualmente en aquel restaurante! ¿Vamos a las ocho?
Maria:	¿A las ocho? Tengo que levantarme temprano...y me ducho esta noche... ¿Prefieres que nos almorcemos?
Ramona:	Posiblemente...Si hace buen tiempo...y tendré que irme para la una.
Maria:	¡Muchas preparaciones para comer! ¿Está este restaurante cercano?
Ramona:	No, este restaurante está en el centro. Conduzco mi coche. Nos vamos para allí a las once y media.
Maria:	Entonces nos almorzamos mañana. ¡Y no tengo que despertarme hasta tarde! ¡Qué bueno!

 Verdadero o falso. Based on the reading, decide if the statements are true or false. Write V or F in the blank.

7.13
   a. _____ The girls are going out for breakfast.

   b. _____ The restaurant is nearby.

   c. _____ They will be leaving the restaurant at 11:30.

   d. _____ They are taking the bus downtown.

   e. _____ Maria is an early riser.

Now the statements are in Spanish!

7.14
   a. _____ Ellas comen el almuerzo.

   b. _____ Cuando llueve mucho, van al restaurante.

   c. _____ Se viste de los pantalones cortos en este restaurante.

   d. _____ Maria tiene que irse del restaurante para la una de la tarde.

   e. _____ A Maria le gusta levantarse tarde.

Answer the following questions in complete Spanish sentences, based on the information from the reading passage.

7.15
   a. ¿Necesitan las muchachas mucho dinero para comer en ese restaurante? ¿Cómo sabes?

b. ¿Dónde está el restaurante?

c. ¿Cómo viajan al restaurante?

d. ¿En tu opinión, qué van a comer María y Ramona para el almuerzo?

e. ¿Por qué prefiere María almorzarse?

Note: This section does not have a Self Test.

LIFEPAC 7: VOCABULARY LIST

El arreglo – Personal:

(las acciónes)

bañarse	to bathe (oneself)
lavarse	to wash (oneself)
cepillarse	to brush (one's hair/teeth)
mirarse	to look at (oneself)
arreglarse	to clean (oneself) up
maquillarse	to put makeup on (oneself)
vestirse (e–i)	to get dressed (dress oneself)
ponerse	to put on (oneself)
quitarse	to take off (oneself)
ducharse	to take a shower
secarse	to dry (oneself) off
ponerse a dieta	to go on a diet
aumentarse de peso	to gain weight
bajarse de peso	to lose weight
dormirse (o–ue)	to fall asleep
acostarse (o–ue)	to go to bed
peinarse	to comb (one's hair)
despertarse (e–ie)	to wake up
levantarse	to get up/to arise
irse	to leave/go out
desayunarse	to eat breakfast
almorzarse(o–ue)	to eat lunch
cenarse	to eat supper
pasearse	to take a walk
correr	to run
decir	to say, tell
dormir	to sleep
ir	to go

(los artículos del arreglo personal)

el jabón	the soap
el champú	the shampoo
el cepillo	the brush
el cepillo de dientes	the toothbrush
el peine	the comb
la ducha	the shower
la bañera	the bathtub
la pasta dentífrica	the toothpaste
el espejo	the mirror

el maquillaje	the makeup
la secadora	the hair dryer
la ropa	the clothes
el zapato	the shoe
la toalla	the towel
el gimnasio	the gym
el desayuno	the breakfast
el almuerzo	the lunch
la cena	the supper
la cama	the bed
el dormitorio	the bedroom
el baño	the bathroom
el reloj	the clock
los dientes	the teeth
el pelo	the hair

El Tiempo:

¿Qué tiempo hace?	How's the weather?
Hace sol.	It's sunny.
Hace frío.	It's cold.
Hace calor.	It's warm/hot.
Hace viento.	It's windy.
Hace buen tiempo.	The weather's good.
Hace mal tiempo.	The weather's bad.
Está nublado.	It's cloudy.
Nieva.	It's snowing.
Llueve.	It's raining.
La temperatura es _____ grados.	The temperature is _____ degrees.
La estación (de)	the season (of)
El invierno	the winter
La primavera	the spring
El verano	the summer
El otoño	the autumn